SAVE OUR ANIMALS!

Bengal Tiger

Louise and Richard Spilsbury

KU-244-325

Heinemann
LIBRARY

www.heinemann.co.uk/library
Visit our website to find out more information about Heinemann Library books.

To order:
 Phone 44 (0) 1865 888066
 Send a fax to 44 (0) 1865 314091
Visit the Heinemann Bookshop at www.heinemann.co.uk/library to browse our catalogue and order online.

First published in Great Britain by Heinemann Library, Halley Court, Jordan Hill, Oxford OX2 8EJ, part of Harcourt Education.
Heinemann is a registered trademark of Harcourt Education Ltd.

© Harcourt Education Ltd 2006
The moral right of the proprietor has been asserted.

All rights reserved. No part of this publication may be reproduced, stored in a retrieval system, or transmitted in any form or by any means, electronic, mechanical, photocopying, recording, or otherwise, without either the prior written permission of the publishers or a licence permitting restricted copying in the United Kingdom issued by the Copyright Licensing Agency Ltd, 90 Tottenham Court Road, London W1T 4LP (www.cla.co.uk).

Editorial: Kate Bellamy, Diyan Leake, Cassie Mayer and Katie Shepherd
Design: Michelle Lisseter and Ron Kamen
Illustrations: Bridge Creative Services
Cartographer: Vickie Taylor at International Mapping
Picture research: Hannah Taylor and Fiona Orbell
Production: Duncan Gilbert

Origination: Chroma Graphics (Overseas) Pte. Ltd
Printed and bound in China by
South China Printing Co. Ltd

The paper used to print this book comes from sustainable resources.

10 digit ISBN 0 431 11422 6
13 digit ISBN 978 0 431 11422 4

10 09 08 07 06
10 9 8 7 6 5 4 3 2 1

DUDLEY PUBLIC LIBRARIES

L

| 715976 | SCH |

J599.744

British Library Cataloguing in Publication Data
Spilsbury, Louise and Richard
Save the Bengal tiger. – (Save our animals!)
599.7' 56
A full catalogue record for this book is available from the British Library.

Acknowledgements
The publishers would like to thank the following for permission to reproduce photographs: Ardea pp. 4 top (Y A Betrand), 5 top left, 14 (J Rajput), 16 (P Morris), 28 (J Daniels); Corbis/Gallo Images p. 29 (M Harvey); Digital Vision p. 5 middle; Ecoscene p. 10 (R Gill); FLPA p. 21 (M Newman); Getty Images/National Geographic pp. 26–27 (J Edwards); Naturepl.com pp. 4 bottom left (M Carwardine), 9 (F Savigny), 17 (K Ammann), 23 (M Birkhead); NHPA p. 25 (M Harvey); Oxford Scientific pp. 4 middle, 5 top right, 6, 7 (M Powles), 11 (M Hill), 13, 22; Panos Pictures p. 18 (A Vitale), 19 (Animals Animals); Reuters p. 12 (D Balibouse); Still Pictures pp. 5 bottom, 15 (A & S Carey); WWF-Canon p. 24 (M Harvey).

Cover photograph of Bengal tiger reproduced with permission of Alamy Images/Mike Hill.

The publishers would like to thank Sarala Khaling at WWF in Nepal for her assistance in the preparation of this book.

Every effort has been made to contact copyright holders of any material reproduced in this book. Any omissions will be rectified in subsequent printings if notice is given to the publishers.

Disclaimer
All Internet addresses (URLs) given in this book were valid at the time of going to press. However, due to the dynamic nature of the Internet, some addresses may have changed or ceased to exist since publication. While the author and the publishers regret any inconvenience this may cause readers, no responsibility for any such changes can be accepted by either the author or the publishers.

Contents

Some words are shown in bold, **like this**. You can find out what they mean by looking in the Glossary.

Animals in trouble

There are many different kinds, or **species**, of animal. Some species are in danger of becoming **extinct**. This means that all the animals from that species might die.

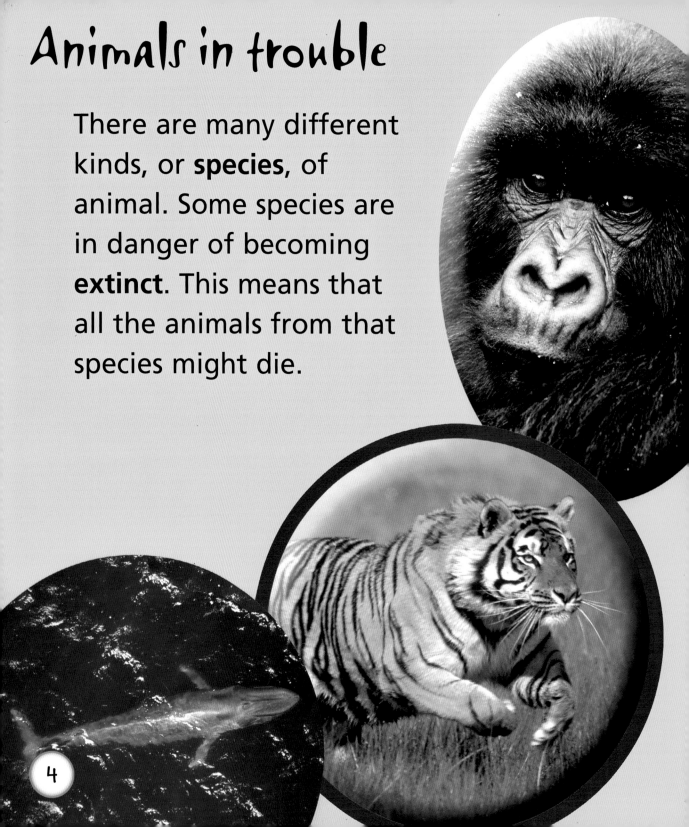

All the animals shown here are in danger of becoming extinct. These species need to be saved. The Bengal tiger is one of them.

The Bengal tiger

Bengal tigers are big animals but they can be hard to spot. Their orange and white hair and dark stripes help them hide in long grass.

It is hard to spot a Bengal tiger in the grass.

Each Bengal tiger has a different pattern of stripes.

Bengal tigers belong to the cat family. Lions, leopards, and cheetahs belong to this family as well. They all have a long tail, big teeth, sharp claws, and a loud roar.

Where can you find Bengal tigers?

You have to travel to **Asia** to find Bengal tigers. Asia is a **continent**. Most Bengal tigers live in parts of India. A few live in other countries near by.

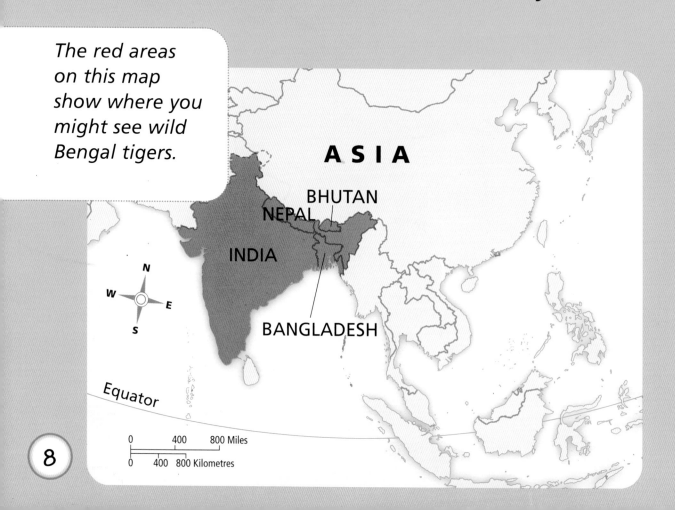

The red areas on this map show where you might see wild Bengal tigers.

ASIA

BHUTAN
NEPAL
INDIA
BANGLADESH

N
W   E
S

Equator

0   400   800 Miles
0   400   800 Kilometres

Where an animal lives is called its **habitat**. Most Bengal tigers' habitat is forests or areas with long grass. Tigers can hide there while they hunt for food.

Bengal tigers prefer to live in wild places, away from people.

What do Bengal tigers eat?

Bengal tigers are **carnivores**, which means they eat meat. Bengal tigers usually hunt pigs, deer, antelopes, or buffalo.

Tigers have sharp teeth for tearing meat.

Tigers need to hunt other animals so that they can eat.

Bengal tigers can hear and see very well. This helps them hunt. A tiger creeps up close behind an animal. Then the tiger runs out to catch it.

Young Bengal tigers

Baby tigers are called **cubs**. **Female** tigers usually have three or four cubs at a time. They give birth in a safe place like a cave.

Tiger cubs are born with their eyes closed.

Bengal tigers are **mammals**. The cubs feed on their mother's milk. Later, their mother will teach them to hunt. After they are two years old, tigers live alone.

Tiger cubs learn hunting skills by playing with each other.

Natural dangers

Tiger **cubs** face dangers in the wild. Hyenas, leopards, and wild dogs can kill them. Some young tigers die because they cannot catch enough food.

Leopards can catch and eat Bengal tiger cubs.

Adult tigers can protect themselves against most animals.

No wild animals hunt adult Bengal tigers. Tigers are too big and strong. Adult tigers die when they get old or wounded in a fight with another tiger.

Hunting and poaching

In the past, people enjoyed hunting Bengal tigers. Indian kings and hunters from Europe rode elephants through the forests. They killed thousands of tigers.

Hunters had photos taken to prove they had killed a tiger.

Poachers hunt tigers and other big cats for their skin.

Today it is against the law to kill Bengal tigers, but some people called **poachers** still do. They sell tiger skins and bones for a lot of money.

Dangers to the Bengal tiger's world

People cut down trees in the tigers' **habitat**. They build homes and farms on the land, so there is no room for the tigers or the animals they eat.

When people live in wild places like this, tigers lose their homes.

There can be problems when people live near tigers. Tigers sometimes hunt farm animals. People chase the tigers away. Sometimes, they kill the tigers.

These men are carrying sticks to scare tigers away from their town.

How many Bengal tigers are there?

In 1900 there were around 100,000 Bengal tigers in Asia. Today, there are only about 4,000 left. The problem is that tigers live alone, in small areas.

Year

1900

2005

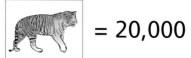 = 20,000

This graph shows how many Bengal tigers there are.

People have built towns and roads in these areas. Now it is hard for tigers to find food, or travel to meet another tiger to **mate**.

People need to keep wild places for the tigers to live in.

How are Bengal tigers being saved?

Some countries have areas of land called **reserves** where tigers are safe and their **habitat** is looked after. People can come and see tigers in reserves.

People pay to visit tigers in reserves. The money goes to guards who protect the tigers.

There are laws to stop people from buying and selling Bengal tiger skins and bones. Police catch **poachers** and punish them for harming Bengal tigers.

These are tiger skins that police took from poachers.

Who is helping Bengal tigers?

Groups of people collect money to pay for Bengal tiger **reserves**. They try to stop people buying medicines made from tiger parts.

Children in school learn how to help save the tigers.

People study tiger footprints to find out where the tigers go.

Some people put radios on tiger collars. These collars show how far tigers travel. Then people know how big the reserves need to be to keep the tigers safe.

How can you help?

It is important to know that Bengal tigers are in danger. Then you can learn how to help save them. Read, watch, and find out all you can about Bengal tigers.

Here are some things you can do to help.

- Join a group such as **WWF**. These groups raise money to protect tigers.
- Visit zoos where tigers live. Some zoos raise money to help wild tigers.

The future for Bengal tigers

The future of the Bengal tiger is uncertain. Some people say that there may be none left in the wild by 2010. Then the only ones we see will be in zoos.

Today there are around 300 Bengal tigers in zoos.

We must all work so that Bengal tigers can live free like this.

Countries must work together to stop people from buying and selling parts of dead tigers. If they are protected, the number of Bengal tigers will grow again.

Bengal tiger facts

- Bengal tigers live to be about 15 years old in the wild.
- A tiger can eat more than your weight in meat in one meal.
- No two tigers have the same stripe patterns. Each tiger's stripes are different.
- There are about 40 white Bengal tigers in zoos across the world. They have cream coloured fur, chocolate coloured stripes, and blue eyes.

More books to read

Bengal Tiger, Edana Eckart (Children's Press, 2003)

Bengal Tiger, Richard Spilsbury (Heinemann, 2004)

Bengal Tiger, Rod Theodorou (Heinemann, 2001)

Websites

To find out more about charities that help tigers, visit their websites:

WWF: www.wwf.org

Save the Tiger: www.savethetigerfund.org

Glossary

Asia   the largest continent in the world

carnivore   animal that eats meat from other animals

continent   large area of land divided into different countries

cub   baby tiger

extinct   when all the animals in a species die out and the species no longer exists

female   animal that can become a mother when it grows up. Women and girls are female people.

habitat   place where plants and animals grow and live. A forest is a kind of habitat.

mammal   animal that feeds its baby with the mother's milk and has some hair on its body

mate   what male and female animals do to make babies

poacher   someone who hunts animals when it is against the law to do so

reserve   area of land where animals are protected and their habitat looked after

species   group of animals that look similar and can have babies together

WWF charity that used to be called the World Wildlife Fund

Index

Titles in the *Save Our Animals!* series include:

Hardback
ISBN 10: 0 431 11421 8
ISBN 13: 978 0 431 11421 7

Hardback
ISBN 10: 0 431 11422 6
ISBN 13: 978 0 431 11422 4

Hardback
ISBN 10: 0 431 11423 4
ISBN 13: 978 0 431 11423 1

Hardback
ISBN 10: 0 431 11424 2
ISBN 13: 978 0 431 11424 8

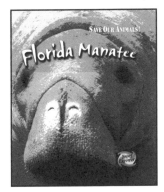

Hardback
ISBN 10: 0 431 11425 0
ISBN 13: 978 0 431 11425 5

Hardback
ISBN 10: 0 431 11426 9
ISBN 13: 978 0 431 11426 2

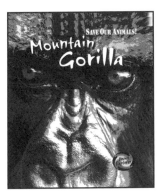

Hardback
ISBN 10: 0 431 11427 7
ISBN 13: 978 0 431 11427 9

Find out about other titles from Heinemann Library on our website www.heinemann.co.uk/library